Copyright: Really Useful Map Company (HK) Ltd.
Published by Robert Frederick Ltd.
4 North Parade Bath, England.
First Published: 2005

DISCOVER BIG CATS

Contents

A Cat's World

Did you know that the common house cat is related to the lions and tigers that you may have seen at the zoo? They are members of the same family called *Felidae*. Each family is special and the curious world of cats is no different.

Meat lovers

Cats are hunters and love meat. Domestic cats hunt for mice, while lions, tigers and jaguars hunt in the wild. They prey on other wild animals for food.

■ The whole world is made up of what are called ecosystems, where living beings live interdependently and feed on one another. The big cats feed on smaller animals like deer, which in turn eat grass and leaves. Such a cycle is called a food chain

■ The king of the jungle is among the mightiest of all big cats

INTERESTING FACT!

Cats have more bones than humans. Humans have only 206 bones in their body, whereas the cat has 230. About 10 per cent of a cat's bones are in its tail. The tail is used to maintain balance.

Tail

On the prowl

They have large eyes, excellent hearing, sharp teeth and strong limbs with sharp claws. This makes them good hunters. Most have long tails and their fur is usually spotted or striped.

■ Big cats have special hunting skills. The jaguar likes to follow its prey before attacking it

FACT FILE

Number of species
36
Smallest cat
rusty-spotted cat stands 17 cm (7 inches) tall and weighs less than 1.5 kg (3 pounds)
Biggest cat
tigers weigh as much as 318 kg (700 pounds) and can be as long as 5 m (14 feet)
Fastest cat
cheetahs can run as fast as 130 km/h (70 mph)
Average life span
15-20 years

Body structure

Most cats have similar skeletons. They have rounded heads and their body structure allows them to move swiftly and silently. Their backbone is very different from humans. While ours is very rigid, the cat's flexible spine allows it to bend into a ball!

Living den

Big cats are native to all continents except Australia and Antarctica. But most of the 36 species of wild cats are in danger. Many scientists believe that many of them may not be around within the next 25 years.

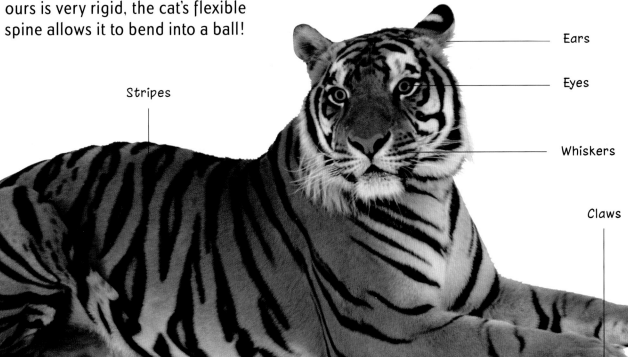

Stripes

Ears

Eyes

Whiskers

Claws

The First Cats

It is a common saying that a cat has nine lives. Although that may not be entirely true, cats have been around for more than 30 million years. While modern cats evolved about 10-12 million years ago, very little is known about their evolution.

First cats

The earliest known cat is the Proailurus ("pro" means old and "ailurus" means cat), which lived about 30 million years ago. It was a small sized animal – the size of a small bobcat – and had a six-inch-long skull. This cat, which is extinct now, had more teeth than its modern cousins.

■ The Proailurus was a strong climber and spent most of its time in trees

Toothy matter

Smilodon, a type of sabre-toothed cat, had long, knife-like front teeth. It used its teeth to cut through the prey's skin, thus wounding it. The prey would then bleed to death. But the Smilodon's teeth were not strong enough to bite into bones and would sometimes break.

■ The sabre-toothed cats had very powerful front legs and a short tail. These cats were not fast runners but followed the prey quietly and sprung a surprise attack on them

Not tigers

The sabre-toothed tiger is yet another prehistoric cat. Despite its name, it is not the ancestors of today's tigers. In fact, this big cat belonged to a separate branch of the cat family that became extinct millions of years ago.

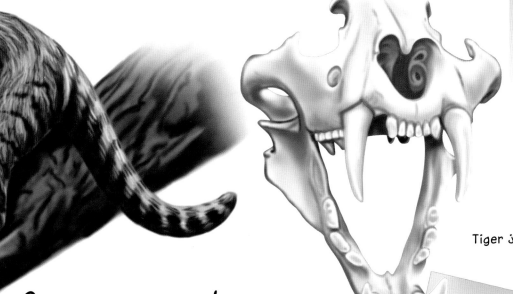

Tiger Jaws

Common ancestor

Among modern cats, jaguars and leopards are believed to have had the same ancestor. But they moved to different areas over the years and developed unique features. Lions, on the other hand, evolved more recently. They were first seen in Western Africa, nearly 750,000 years ago and then spread into Asia, Europe and America.

INTERESTING FACT!

The sabre-toothed tiger probably lived on grassy plains and open woodlands, in and around North and South America. It lived in the last ice age, about 1.5 million years ago. They were the main predators of the time.

■ Early forms of the cheetah are also believed to have inhabited North America as far back as 2.5 million years ago. Some scientists believe that cheetahs have ancestral links with the puma

Cat Family

Cats in the wild have been classified as small, medium and large depending on their size. They are also divided into three groups based on their traits. These are *Felinae*, *Pantherinae* and *Acinonychinae*.

Domestic vs wild

Domestic cats and their wild relatives share many characteristics. They have short, strong jaws and sharp teeth. All cats are good hunters. But while smaller cats like to eat standing, big cats like to lie down and eat their food.

■ Domestic cats hold their tails low and swing them to indicate that they are feeling playful or nervous. An upright tail is usually a sign of alertness. Big cats too behave similarly

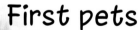

■ The polecat has a long, slender body and short legs. It feeds on rats, mice, rabbits, fish, eggs and fruit but, despite its misleading name, is not a member of the cat family.

First pets

Archaeological studies show that human beings have kept pet cats for nearly 8,000 years. In Egypt, 4,000 years ago, they were kept because of their skill to hunt snakes, rats and mice. The Egyptians also worshipped cats and believed they were forms of the Goddess Bast. It was a crime to kill cats or trade in them.

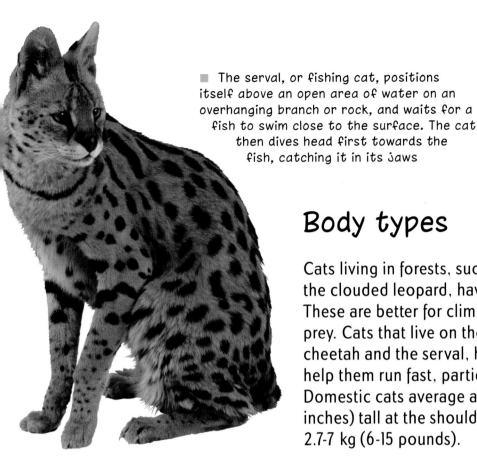

■ The serval, or fishing cat, positions itself above an open area of water on an overhanging branch or rock, and waits for a fish to swim close to the surface. The cat then dives head first towards the fish, catching it in its jaws

Body types

Cats living in forests, such as the jaguar and the clouded leopard, have short, stocky limbs. These are better for climbing trees and ambushing prey. Cats that live on the savannah, such as the cheetah and the serval, have long limbs. These help them run fast, particularly when chasing prey. Domestic cats average about 20-25 cm (8-10 inches) tall at the shoulder and weigh from 2.7-7 kg (6-15 pounds).

Purr and meow

Some scientists say a domestic cat can make more than 60 different sounds and they may have different meanings. For example, a meow can be a friendly greeting, or it may express curiosity, hunger, or loneliness. Purring usually means contentment, but some cats also purr when they are sick. Hisses, growls, and screams indicate anger and fear.

INTERESTING FACT!

Despite its name, the polecat is actually a member of the weasel family and is related to the skunk and the ferret. Similarly, the Australian tiger cat is a marsupial that is closely related to the possum and the Tasmanian Devil.

■ Different types of cats can be cross-bred to give rise to new breeds, or hybrids. The liger, one of the most well-known hybrids, is obtained by inter-breeding a lion and a tiger

Cat Senses

These specialist hunters rely on their senses of sight and hearing to locate their prey. They also produce a wide range of sounds, including snarls, growls, purrs and roars. While lions and tigers roar, cheetahs and pumas tend to purr.

Looking afar

Big cats have excellent day and night vision. Their eyes face forward, allowing both eyes to focus on the same object. Their sharp eyesight allows them to judge distances and the size of the object as well.

■ Apart from its strong muscles and teeth, a tiger also relies on its senses for a successful hunt

Vision at night

The big cat's eye is larger than a human's. A cat has a larger pupil, which allows more light to enter the eye at night. While a human pupil is always circular, the cat can shrink its pupil from a circle into a slit like opening. It does so in bright sunlight, allowing less light to enter the eye.

INTERESTING FACT!

No one knows exactly how a cat sees colour, but they definitely do not see it the way we do. According to most scientists, reds appear darker, while greens appear much lighter and duller to a cat.

A pair of glowing eyes can look scary at night.

Moving ears

Cats have very sharp hearing and can pinpoint the location of a sound almost immediately. The ear has nearly 20 muscles attached to it. The moment a cat hears a sound, it can move its ears in that direction.

Pinnae

■ The external ears of cats are shaped like a cup and are called pinnae

■ Cats like tigers can smell the presence of another cat that has left its scent in a marked area

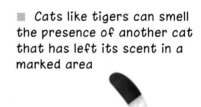

Marked territory

All cats have marked areas where they live, and other cats are not allowed into them. These usually include hunting grounds, dens, water spots and resting spots. Big cats mark these territories to warn other cats. They leave their scent by spraying urine in special locations or by scratching on trees. They can also leave their scent by rubbing their chins, cheeks, and tails onto objects.

Of Fur and Claws

Big cats are covered with fur. The fur coat protects the animal in very cold or hot weather. But more importantly, the unique pattern on it acts as camouflage. Camouflage is the ability of an animal to blend with its surroundings. This makes them nearly invisible!

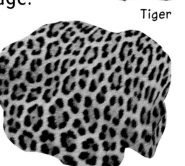

■ Cats have different patterns on their coats depending on the habitat in which they live

Tiger

Leopard

Cheetah

Protective coat

Just as you wear woollen jumpers in the winter, big cats living in cold areas have thick fur to protect them from the cold. The snow leopard has long, woolly fur which is longer on the animal's belly. This gives extra protection to the part of the body closest to the snow-covered ground. Cats living in warmer climates have short, bristly fur.

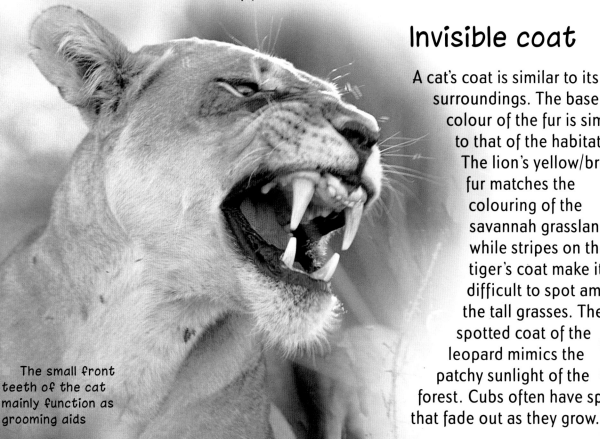

The small front teeth of the cat mainly function as grooming aids

Invisible coat

A cat's coat is similar to its surroundings. The base colour of the fur is similar to that of the habitat. The lion's yellow/brown fur matches the colouring of the savannah grasslands while stripes on the tiger's coat make it difficult to spot among the tall grasses. The spotted coat of the leopard mimics the patchy sunlight of the forest. Cubs often have spots that fade out as they grow.

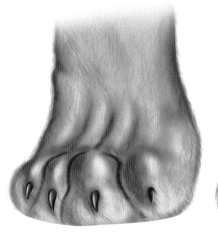

■ Apart from a cheetah, all cats have retractable claws.
These claws are inside the paws, and come out only during attacks

Death grip

Claws are a very important hunting
tool for cats. Apart from the cheetah,
all cat claws stay covered in their paws.
This keeps them safe and sharp. Their
claws help the big cats to climb trees,
and are also handy while attacking a
prey or defending themselves.

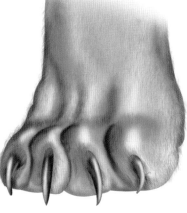

INTERESTING FACT!

Long fur is not just to
protect against the cold. The
black-footed cat and sand cat
both have longer fur covering
their feet and pads. Both
these cats live in desert areas,
and the fur protects against
the heat of the ground.

Vanity fare

The tongue of the wild cat is much rougher
than that of the domestic cat. Its surface is
covered with tiny hooks that helps the cat to
clean and comb its fur. It also helps them to
strip flesh off the bones of their prey.

■ An adult mountain lion may be either
grey or reddish-yellow in colour. It does
not have any spots

Young Ones

Big cats, like human beings, give birth to their young. While a domestic cat's young are called kittens, a big cat's young are called cubs. The mother usually takes care of her cubs till they grow older and can look after themselves. Cubs, like human babies, are quite helpless at birth. Some are even born blind!

Born weak

The mother moves her cubs from one hiding place to another to protect them. She carries them in her mouth, one at a time. Hyenas, leopards, and even other lions may kill cubs while the mother is away hunting.

Food habits

For the first month and a half, the cubs live only on their mother's milk. When they are older, the mother leads them to an animal she has killed. Cats look after their young ones till they are about 18 to 24 months old – when they can hunt for themselves.

■ The lioness carries a cub in her mouth, holding it by the neck. Lion cubs have a thick padding on their necks, which prevents the mother's teeth from injuring them

■ Cubs depend on their mother's milk for about three to six months

One-year-old cubs accompany their mothers on a hunt

FACT FILE

Tiger litter
2-4 cubs
Lion litter
1-6 cubs
Cheetah litter
3-5 cubs
Size of a tiger cub
1.5 kg (3 pounds)
Size of a cougar cub
0.5 kg (1 pound)

INTERESTING FACT!

Cubs chase each other and wrestle as they practise some of the skills they will need in their adult life. Sometimes the mother leads the prey to her cubs, so that they can practice their hunting skills.

School time

The mother cat usually trains her cubs to hunt after their first year. She does this by bringing them live animals to catch and kill. The cub begins its training by mimicking the mother.

Cheetahs hide their cubs in tree tops to protect them from predators

Special babies

In zoos, big cats can have special cubs, where the father may be a lion and the mother a tiger. Such cubs are called tiglons, tigons, or ligers.

Attack

The cat's body is perfectly built for hunting and killing. It has strong grasping limbs, sharp claws, and knife-like canine teeth. Most cats hunt at dawn or dusk and have excellent senses of vision and hearing. They often have patterned coats that help hide them from their prey.

■ The stripes on a tiger's body allows it to hide in the grass from its prey

Run and pounce

When the cat senses the right moment, it transfers its bodyweight to its rear legs and lunges towards the victim. This begins the chase. If the cat was close enough, the prey's run is short. The final phase is the pounce. The cat grabs the animal, and pulls it to the ground. Then it suffocates its prey with its mouth and kills it.

Stalk and ambush

Stalking is when the cat follows its prey silently before attacking. A hunting technique used when a cat hides and attacks suddenly is called an ambush. If an unsuspecting animal comes within striking distance, it comes out of hiding and lunges toward its surprised and unprepared victim.

The Lioness is the main hunter in a group, although she is helped by her bigger cubs. The lion only joins in when the prey is big

■ While cats approach very quietly, the prey is often alerted by other herd members. The entire herd then breaks into a run

Final kill

All cats do not kill their prey in the same way. Small cats kill their prey with a bite to the back of the neck. Large cats suffocate their prey, either with a stranglehold on the neck or by covering the prey's snout with their jaws.

Success rate

The cheetah is the best hunter within the wild cat species. It catches up to 60-70 per cent of prey that it hunts. The lion on the other hand has a low success rate at less than 30 per cent.

INTERESTING FACT!

Some cats like the caracal use their paws to catch birds. Just as the bird takes flight, the cat rises up on its hind legs, jumps up and catches its prey with an extended paw. Having caught the bird in both paws, it brings it down and eats it.

■ Among the hunting techniques the cheetah specialises in, is the final run. Several physical features allow the cheetah to run faster than any other land animal

Defence

While big cats are known to be the most deadly predators, many have had to develop methods to protect themselves from injury during a hunt. They also face threats from other cats who may take over their territory or try and steal their kill from them. Protecting the cubs is the responsibility of the female.

■ A leopard will climb a tree to protect its kill from other animals like lions and hyenas who have been known to steal their prey from them

In the family

A lioness will protect her cubs from other animals and also from lions who pose a threat to them. When a new male lion takes over a pride, he usually kills all the cubs and mates with the lionesses to start his own family. The male lion protects the entire family and his mane makes him look larger to other lions.

Group attack

Lions usually hunt together to increase their chances of killing prey and protecting themselves. They fan out in a semicircle to creep up on the prey. Lions have been known to be injured while hunting larger prey, like giraffes and elephants.

■ A lioness defends the young ones in the pride. It will attack any wild animal that could harm her cubs

FACT FILE

**Special features
for hunting**
The serval has large
and sensitive ears. It can
even detect its prey
burrowing beneath the
surface of the ground
A cat is
three times more sensitive
to sound than a human.
A cat can completely rotate
its ears to the left or right
right following a sound

Defending territory

Big cats like tigers are very protective of
their territory. One male's territory generally
includes three to four females. Males will
aggressively fight each other to defend their
territory. However, neighbouring females have
been known to share their kill.

Animal attack

Other animals also have unique methods of defending
themselves against the mighty cats. Elephants kick,
rampage, trample and usually succeed in running
away. Zebras snort loudly to alert the herd of
impending danger. The males will position themselves
between the predator and the herd and kick and
bite giving the herd time to escape. Animals like the
wildebeest are known to break into a stampede.

INTERESTING FACT!

Some cats attack in groups.
A few cats act as 'beaters',
moving openly toward an
intended victim and driving it
in the direction of another
cat lying in wait, ready to
pounce. This strategy is used
by both lynx and lion.

■ When a herd of elephants face
danger, the adults form a circle
around the calves to protect
them. Big cats, however, rarely
attack elephants because of
their sheer size difference

King of Savannahs

The lion is called the king of beasts, because it is big and powerful. The male lion has a mane around its neck that adds to its royal look. And its loud roar is fierce and frightening. Lions are truly majestic and they make no bones about it.

Living in the open

Unlike tigers, lions don't like living in thick forests. They would rather roam through open lands, and are usually found in woodlands, grassy plains, and areas with thorny scrub trees. Lions live where they find a steady supply of food like deer, antelope, zebra, and other hoofed animals. Lions also need to live near water.

In zoos and in the wild

Lions are found in eastern and southern Africa. A few hundred can be found in the Gir Forest of India. They are called Asiatic lions. Most lions live in national parks and areas called reserves, where the animals are protected from hunters. Hundreds of lions also live in zoos and are extremely popular performers in circuses.

■ Lion cubs can be tamed easily. Circuses start training lions when they are about two years old

Lion´s mane

Lions are better known for their strength, not speed. Male lions are the only cats with manes. This collar of long, thick hair covers the head, except the face, and the neck down to the shoulders and chest. The mane makes the male look bigger and stronger.

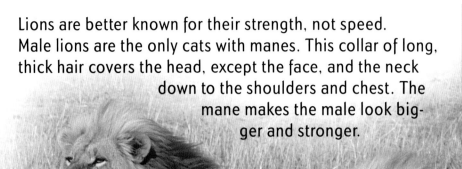

FACT FILE

Average weight is about 160-180 kg (353-397 pounds). A large male can weigh up to 230 kg (507 pounds)
As long as 3 m (10 feet)
Stands at 1 m (3.2 feet) tall at the shoulder
The weight of a lioness is about 110-140 kg (243-309 pounds)
Lionesses are nearly 30 cm (1 foot) shorter than lions

INTERESTING FACT!

The lion's mane protects him during fights. The long, thick hair softens the enemy's blows. One year old cubs have little hair around their heads. The mane is not fully grown until the animal is about 5 years old.

■ Unlike most wild cats who prefer to live alone, lions love living in one big family

Colouring matter

The lion's coat is ideal for hiding while on a hunt. It is a brownish yellow – the same colour as dead grass. Only the back of the ears and the tuft of hair at the end of the tail are black. Cubs have spots on their coats.

☐ The male lions in the pride ordinarily let the lionesses do the hunting for the family. But they kill for themselves when they find prey

Living in Prides

Lions are the only big cats that live in a group, called a pride. A pride usually has 10 to 20 lions. A large pride may have as many as 35 lions. Each pride can have from one to five adult males, several lionesses, and cubs. Members of a pride stay together as a family. When they meet, they greet each other by rubbing cheeks.

■ While lions can climb trees if they have to, most of them avoid it. They are simply too heavy

Marked area

All male cubs are chased from the territory by their fathers when they are between 2 and 3 years old. These young males then wander until they form their own pride. Each pride stays in a specific area called its territory. Lions do not allow strange predators to hunt in their territory.

Strong muscles

A lion's legs and shoulders are very muscular. They give the lion the strength to clutch its prey and pull it to the ground. Each paw has curved claws that hook and hold the prey. When not in use, each claw withdraws into the paw so the claws stay sharp.

■ Lions usually spend about 20 hours a day sleeping or resting. Hungry cubs can be nursed by any lioness that has milk and not just their own mothers

Gulping food

The lion has 30 teeth. The four large pointed teeth are used to hold the prey, kill it, and to tear the meat. Four cheek teeth are used for cutting through the prey's tough skin and muscles. But the lion has no teeth for chewing. It swallows the food in chunks.

FACT FILE

Territory spread over
40-260 sq km
(15-100 sq miles)
Cubs weigh
1.5 kg (3 pounds) at birth
Lion's top speed
is about 55 km/h (34 mph)
Can travel as far as
24 km (15 miles) in
search of food
A male lion can
eat 35 kg (77 pounds) of
meat in one meal

■ A lot of animals like this African hunting dog and hyenas feed on the leftovers of lions

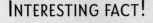

INTERESTING FACT!

The Asiatic lion has a thicker coat and a more pronounced fringe of hair on its belly compared to the African lion. The tassel at the end of the Asiatic lion's tail is also considerably larger. However, its mane is much smaller.

■ Masai warriors are nomadic people, who live in Kenya. In the past, young men from the tribe had to kill a lion to prove that they were mature and strong. Today, this practice has been made illegal

In danger

The Asiatic lion is an endangered species. African lions have a much better chance for survival. Africa has many reserves where lions may not be shot. The lion tries to avoid contact with people. It rarely attacks humans unless it is threatened, tormented or injured.

The Tiger Trail

The tiger is the largest member of the cat family. After the lion, tigers are perhaps the most awesome of all the big cats. In the old days, kings would hunt tigers for their beautiful fur. The large scale killing of tigers and clearing of forests have left just a few thousands of them in the wild today. The tiger lives in the forests of Asia and is part of many a myth and story!

■ Tigers are extremely fast when running short distances and can leap nearly 9 m (30 feet). But if a tiger fails to catch its prey quickly, it will give up the moment it feels tired

Striped giants

Tigers can be easily recognised because of their striped fur and skin. They usually have an orange or brownish yellow coat with a white chest and belly. Their coat is covered with broken vertical black/dark brown stripes. These stripes allow the animal to blend in while walking through tall grass.

Living in shadows

Tigers live in oak wood forests, tall grasslands, swamps and marshes. They are found in the hot rainforests of Malaya, the dry thorn woods of India and the cold, snowy spruce forests of northern China. Tigers rarely go into open spaces like lions do.

■ A tiger marks its territory with urine, claw marks, or by rubbing its tail against a tree or a rock. The scent and mark let other tigers know that the territory is occupied

On the prowl

The tiger usually hunts at night, following animal trails along stream beds. A tiger uses its sharp eyes and keen ears for a hunt, along with its sense of smell. The tiger waits in cover, before rushing at its prey and leaping at it. Using its sharp claws, the tiger grasps its victim by the side and pulls it to the ground.

Tigers are good swimmers and they enjoy wading in water, especially when it gets hot. Tigers can climb trees, but they do not usually do so because of their huge size

Hearty meal

A tiger can go without food for a long time after a successful hunt. The tiger stays near the carcass until it has eaten everything except its bones and stomach. A tiger may eat over 40 kg (88 pounds) of meat in a night, gulping in the food rather than chewing it. A long drink and a nap often follow a meal.

INTERESTING FACT!

Adult tigers usually live alone, but they are not unsociable. Two tigers may meet on their nightly rounds. They rub heads together in a kind of greeting and then part ways. Tigers have also been known to share a kill as well.

■ Tigers prefer large prey, such as deer, antelope, wild oxen and wild pigs. Some tigers also attack elephant calves. Tigers especially like porcupines, but their quills cause them painful wounds

Tigers in Danger!

There are eight sub-species of tiger. These are the Bali tiger, Bengal tiger, Caspian tiger, Indo-Chinese tiger, Javan tiger, Siberian tiger, South China tiger, and Sumatran tiger. Of these, the Bali tiger, Caspian tiger and Javan tiger are now extinct. The remaining five are also in danger of becoming extinct.

One family

The Indo-Chinese tiger is found in Thailand, south China, Myanmar, Cambodia, Vietnam and parts of Malaysia. These tigers are one of the smaller sub-species. The Siberian tiger is found in Russia and is the largest of all tiger species. The Sumatran tiger is only found on the Indonesian island of Sumatra. It is the smallest of all the tiger species. The South Chinese tiger is considered to be the evolutionary ancestor of all the other tiger sub-species. This tiger is the world's most endangered species.

■ The tigers of Siberia, where the winters are bitterly cold, have long, shaggy, winter coats

Just a few

There are fewer than 200 Siberian tigers in the wild and they are found mainly in Russia. The South China tiger is even rarer. Demand for tiger parts like the eyes, bones and skin for use in traditional Chinese medicine led to an increase in poaching after the 1980s. This has threatened the tiger with extinction.

Man eaters?

There are many tales about Great Bengal Tigers being ferocious man-eaters. Yet almost all wild tigers avoid people. Probably only three or four out of every 1,000 tigers eat people. Most man-eaters are sick or wounded animals that can no longer hunt large, fast-footed prey.

FACT FILE

Great Bengal Tiger
3,030-4,735
Siberian Tiger
160-230
South China Tiger
20-50
Sumatran Tiger
400-500
Indo-Chinese Tiger
1,180-1,790

INTERESTING FACT!

Many adult males claim a territory as their own and keep other males out. The territory may average about 52 sq km (20 square miles) and usually includes a water body. Tigers also communicate by using different sounds.

■ In the Sunderban Reserve, along the coast of the Bay of Bengal in India, tigers are reported to have attacked people. Since tigers are thought to attack only from the rear, the people here wear masks on the backs of their heads. This second "face" is thought to confuse the tigers and thus protect the wearer

White Bengal tigers

Some tigers have chalk-white fur with chocolate-brown or black stripes. These tigers are called white tigers and they have blue eyes. All other tigers have yellow eyes. White tigers are very rare in the wild. More than 100 white tigers live in the world's zoos.

■ White tigers are a variant of Bengal tigers and are rarely found in the wild anymore. A normal-coloured female can give birth to a litter in which some of the cubs are white

Leopards

Leopards are the third largest among big cats, after tigers and lions. They are excellent climbers and, unlike most other wild cats, love living in trees. These cats can in live in various kinds of habitat and also have a wide range of prey. They live in the Saharan regions of Africa, and many Asian countries like Turkey, Korea, Java and India.

Leopards spend most of their lives on tree tops

Clear markings

The leopard is most easily recognised by its rosette patterned coat and extremely long tail which is darker than the rest of its body. The base colour of the coat varies according to the leopard's habitat. Leopards living in open grasslands are golden yellow, while those found in deserts are yellow or cream in colour. Leopards living in mountain regions are deep gold in colour.

Night hunter

Leopards usually hunt at night, though females with cubs prefer to hunt during the day. These cats hunt all kinds of prey, be it impalas, gazelles, hares, reptiles, small monkeys and various rodents such as rats, squirrels and porcupines.

Clouded leopards have cloud-like spots on their skin. Found in south eastern Asia, they often hang upside down from tree branches!

FACT FILE

Can grow as long as
2.5 m (8 feet)
Can be as tall as
70 cm (2 feet)
Average weight
30-90 kg
(66-198 pounds)
Litter Size
1-4 on average
Life Span
12-17 years

Strong and mean

Leopards have very strong muscles and can carry a fully grown male antelope or even a young giraffe – weighing up to three times its own body weight – high into the tree tops. Leopards are also known to attack humans and their livestock, and can be more dangerous than tigers or lions.

■ Snow leopards, found in the snow capped mountains of Russia, China and the Himalayas, have woolly furs. Interestingly, their voice is weak and they cannot roar like other big cats

Killed for fur

But humans have also been a threat to these cats. They have killed leopards for their fur. As a result leopards have become rare in many places. Many countries have banned trade in leopard skins to protect the animal.

INTERESTING FACT!

All black leopards, sometimes called 'Black Panthers' are found in the dense, wet forested areas of India and Southeast Asia. Their dark colour gives them an advantage while hunting.

■ Vervet monkeys make a loud barking call when a leopard is near to alert the rest of their group

The Swiftest

The fastest animal on the earth, the cheetah is unique in many ways. It looks like a large muscular greyhound, with a sleek body and long, thin but powerful legs. This gives the big cat great speed while on the chase. A fully-grown cheetah can reach speeds greater than 113 km/h (70 mph) – which is as fast as a sports car!

■ Cheetahs live in dry areas like bush lands, savannah and semi-deserts and feed on gazelles, impala, wildebeest and zebra

Following prey

The cheetah hunts mainly by day. It first follows a large herd of gazelle, impala or antelope from a distance. It then selects old, injured or young animals as its prey. The cheetah then chases the animal. The cheetah usually catches its prey in the first attempt.

The kill

The cheetah's powerful jaw muscles enable the cat to grip its prey for several minutes and suffocate the animal by clamping the windpipe. The cheetah has enlarged nasal passages, which enables it to breathe more easily while on the run.

■ Once the kill has been made the cheetah pauses to regain its breath. But at this time, hyenas can attack the big cat and snatch its prey away

■ The cheetah's paws are like a dog's. They are narrow and hard padded and, unlike other big cats, cheetah's claws do not go in. This allows it to grip the land better while running

HABITAT

FACT FILE

Can be as long as
1-1.5 m (3-5 feet)
Can be as tall as
1 m (3 feet)
Average weight
45-65 kg
(99-143 pounds)
Litter Size
2-4 cubs
Life Span
12-14 years

Solitary beings

Most adult cheetahs live alone. Wild cheetahs may claim a territory as their own and keep other cheetahs out.

INTERESTING FACT!

Unlike other big cats, the cheetah does not roar. It purrs and can even make other vocal sounds ranging from high pitched yelps and barks to longer chirruping sounds. They can also moan and bleat.

Numbers fall

Cheetahs were commonly found in India and the southern tip of Africa. But their numbers have fallen sharply, and the cat is now confined to sub-Saharan Africa and a small population in Iran. Not only are cheetahs hunted by humans, their young ones are also often killed by lions. In fact, only one in 20 survive to adulthood.

Jaguars of America

Jaguars are often confused with leopards. Both have a similar brownish/yellow base fur colour, with dark rosette markings. But jaguars can be spotted because of the small dots or irregular shapes within the larger rosette markings. They are more stocky and muscular and have a shorter tail.

Living zone

The jaguar is the biggest cat found in the Americas. Jaguars once inhabited areas between the southern states of the U.S. down to the tip of South America. But their population is now limited to the north and central parts of South America. These big cats prefer to live in forest areas, though they can be spotted around dry woodland and grasslands.

Black jaguars are often wrongly called black panthers or black leopards. But a good way to identify them is by their large head and stocky forelimbs

Great variety

The body of a jaguar often depends on its habitat. Those living in dense forested areas are smaller than the ones living in open areas. The forest dwellers are also darker in colour for better camouflage.

Females keep their cubs safe in caves, rocky dens or holes in the forest floor

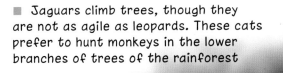

■ Jaguars climb trees, though they are not as agile as leopards. These cats prefer to hunt monkeys in the lower branches of trees of the rainforest

HABITAT

FACT FILE

Can be as long as
1.5-2.5 m (5-8 feet)
Average weight
70-120 kg
(154-265 pounds)
Litter Size
1-4 cubs
Life Span
12-16 years
Size of cub
0.7-1 kg
(1.5-2 pounds)

In danger

There was a sharp fall in the jaguar population in the 1960s and 1970s. As many as 18,000 jaguars were killed every year for their coats. While jaguar fur is no longer in fashion, the big cat is still under threat. Many organisations are trying to protect the animal and the forests where they live.

INTERESTING FACT!

Jaguars are revered in many ancient cultures. The Mayans believed that Jaguar, the god of the underworld, helped the sun to travel under the earth at night, making sure that it rose again the following morning.

Munching time

Even its hunting habits vary according to its habitat. If they live close to humans, jaguars hunt at night. Jaguars that live in the wild prefer to hunt during the day. They hunt cattle, horses, deer, reptiles, monkeys and even fish.

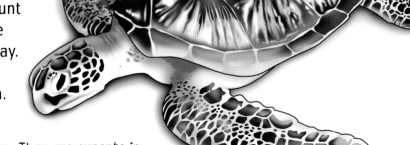

■ Jaguars like to live close to water. They are experts in catching fish and will often tackle turtles, dragging them out from the water and crushing their shells with their powerful jaws

Lynx and Ocelot

Not all big cats are as huge as lions, tigers or leopards. Lynxes and ocelots are much smaller in size but that does not make them any less awesome. Both these animals are good hunters. But, like most big cats, they too are in danger of extinction.

■ A young ocelot can be tamed and makes an excellent pet

Hungry lynx

Lynxes live in parts of Africa, Asia, Europe, and North America. They prefer to stay in forests or in rocky, brush-covered places. They hunt mainly at night and feed on rabbits and other small animals. A hungry lynx can even kill fox and deer.

Spots and stripes

The lynx's fur grows long all over its body. The fur is light grey or greyish brown, long and silky. It is spotted and striped with a darker shade. Lynxes have stubby tails and long tufts of hair on their pointed ears.

■ The lynx has huge feet with thick fur cover. These act as snowshoes and help it run swiftly over snow in winter. Lynxes sleep in caves or hollow trees. They like to climb trees and lie on the branches

Dots galore

The ocelot's fur colour varies from reddish-yellow to smoky-pearl in colour. Its body is covered with black spots of different sizes. The spots on its legs and feet are like dots, while other body parts can have shell-shaped spots. The ocelot has a pink nose and large, translucent eyes.

■ Although similar in appearance to the lynx, the bobcat has relatively shorter legs and smaller paws

Meal time

The ocelot is also known as the leopard cat or tiger cat of the U.S. The ocelot lives in an area ranging from Texas to northern Argentina. It eats mice, wood rats, rabbits, snakes, lizards, birds, young deer and monkeys.

■ Ocelots are widely hunted for their fur and their numbers have decreased sharply. There are now laws to stop the killing of ocelots

INTERESTING FACT!

The African lynx is called the caracal. It mainly inhabits the desert and mountainous regions of southern Africa, but it is now rare. The caracal is also found in Asia.

Pumas

A cat of many names, the Puma is also known as the cougar, panther or mountain lion. It is found in Canada, North America and parts of South America. The puma has a small, broad head with small rounded ears. The cat's body is powerful, with long hind legs and a tail with a black tip.

■ Pumas have from one to five cubs at a time, generally two years apart. The average number is three

Coats of many colours

An adult puma may be either grey or reddish-yellow in colour. Its fur is fawn-grey tipped with reddish-brown or greyish colour. This animal has no spots. This is one of the differences between a puma and a jaguar. They can also be solid black in colour.

Hunting skills

While on the hunt, the puma uses the strength of its powerful back legs to lunge at its prey with a single jump while it is still running. A puma can pounce over 12 m (40 feet).

■ A puma keeps under cover while stalking its prey. It then pounces, breaking its prey's neck or dragging it down to the ground

FACT FILE

Average length
more than 1.5 m (5 feet)
Can be as heavy as
103 kg (227 pounds)
The male is 1.4 times
the size of the female
Life span
10 to 20 years
Cubs weigh
0.5 kg (1 pound)
at birth

■ Pumas teach their young by taking them on hunts. The cub observes how the mother stalks and finally kills the prey

Variety of food

The puma hunts alone, by day or night and will hide its food in dense undergrowth, returning to it over several days. Large prey like elk may provide food for over a week. The puma can tackle larger prey such as domestic cattle or horses. The killing of livestock is one the main reasons that man hunts the puma. They also hunt wild deer, sheep, rodents, rabbits, hare, porcupines, squirels, insects, fish and beavers.

INTERESTING FACT!

The cry of the mountain lion can be very scary. Unlike the deep roar of the African or Asiatic lion, it is shrill and sounds like a human being screaming. The puma can also roar softly. This sounds like a soft whistle.

Numbers dropping

Widespread hunting and trapping by humans has led to a drop in the number of pumas in the wild. The Florida panther, a kind of puma, is in great danger. Only 50 of these pumas are living in the wild today. Pumas shy away from human beings and are unlikely to attack them.

Closest Relatives

Big cats are not the only predators roaming the jungles. These cats have many close relatives like the hyena and civet. These animals might not look like cats, but they are, in fact, close relatives of cats.

Cat-like looks

The civet is a furry animal that looks somewhat like a long, slender cat. But a civet has a more pointed snout, a fluffier tail, and shorter legs than a cat. Their fur may be black, brown, grey, or tan and can even have dark spots. Civets live in Asia and in Africa. They feed on mice, rats, chickens and raid fruit orchards.

■ The cat family is made up of many different kinds of animals. Be it the domestic cat or those in the wild, all are related

■ The caracal is a member of the cat family and is related to the lynx. Like the lynx, the caracal also has tufts of long hair on the tips of its ears. The lynx has brown tufts, but the caracal's are black

INTERESTING FACT!

Hyenas can crack bones with their strong jaws and sharp teeth. They also have very strong digestive systems and can eat bones, teeth, tough skin, and horn! Hyenas can live without drinking water for many days.

Not a dog!!

Although they look more like dogs, hyenas actually belong to the cat family. Hyenas can be spotted, striped or brown in colour. They hunt animals like zebras, gazelles, and buffaloes for food. They also eat the remains of animals they find dead. Often a lion steals hunted animals from a hyena!

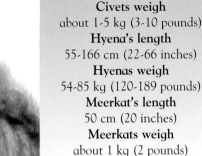

■ The spotted hyena has a very scary cry. It sounds like loud hysterical laughter. These animals are often called laughing hyenas

Living in clans

Like lions, hyenas also live in groups or clans. These clans have hierarchy, which means one animal is superior to the other. The higher animal gets the best share of food and care. Young hyenas are very aggressive and twins begin to fight immediately after birth. Unlike other cubs, hyenas are strong at birth with open eyes and sharp canines.

Similar sounding

Meerkats are not cats as their name suggests but a type of mongoose found in African grasslands. The meerkat is a good hunter. It eats bugs, lizards, and small rodents. Unlike most mongoose, meerkats live in large groups – very much like lions and hyenas.

■ Meerkats live in burrows and tunnels made in the ground. Meerkats watch out for each other, and are often seen on their hind feet with their noses in the air, looking around

Endangered Cats

Though big cats are powerful and strong animals, their survival is threatened today. Over the past one hundred years, there has been a sharp fall in their numbers. Many types of these beautiful animals have become endangered. This means that their numbers have fallen so much that none might be left, if they are not protected.

Loss of territory

The biggest threat to cats is a loss of their natural homes. As humans continue to cut down forests and clear grasslands, these animals are left with very few places to live in. And to make matters worse, humans also hunt these animals, leading to a further loss of lives.

Priceless parts

Hunting big cats was a favourite sport for many kings and lords in the past. These animals are also hunted for their skin, fur and body parts. These items often sell for a high price in the market.

In China and Far East Asia, organs and bones of tigers and leopards are used in special medicinal potions

■ In the last 100 years the tiger population has fallen by half. There are very few tigers left on the planet

FACT FILE

Recently extinct cats
Indian cheetah, the Bali, Javan and Caspian tigers, Taiwanese clouded leopard, Alpine lynx
Endangered cats
lynx, snow leopard, tiger, Florida cougar, Asiatic cheetah, Asiatic lion, Arabian leopards, sand cat

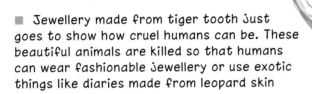

■ Jewellery made from tiger tooth just goes to show how cruel humans can be. These beautiful animals are killed so that humans can wear fashionable jewellery or use exotic things like diaries made from leopard skin

Saving grace

Many organisations have taken steps to protect the big cats. Special areas or reserves have been made for these animals where they can be safe. Zoos are developing ways to make sure the cats have more babies. Many countries have also put a stop to the sale of furs and body parts of most endangered wild cats.

Project tiger

One of the largest projects started to protect big cats was Project Tiger. It began in the 1970s in India. The project led to the opening of nine tiger reserves, which soon increased to 20. These reserves made sure the tigers had a safer place to live in.

INTERESTING FACT!

The clouded leopard is hunted for its skin and its teeth. In Asian markets, these are sold as decorations, while the bones are used to make medicines. Some restaurants in Thailand and China serve clouded leopard meat.

Glossary

Adapt: To change to be able to live in a new situation

Ambush: Hiding and waiting to attack someone by surprise

Ancestors: A member of your family who lived long before your grandparents

Archaeology: The scientific study of fossils and monuments of life and activities in ancient times

Beaters: Someone who strikes bushes or other hiding places to make prey move

Camouflage: The ability to hide or blend in with one's surroundings

Carcass: The body of a dead animal

Classify: Divide based on special characteristics

Domestic: Living near or in human habitation

Ecosystems: Different beings living in one environment, depending on each other and working together

Endangered: Those species that are in danger of becoming extinct

Evolution: A slow process of change where a living being changes from a simple to a more complex creature

Extinct: A species that has been wiped out of existence

Felidae: The family to which all cats belong. The name feline comes from this word

Food chain: The system in where larger animals feed on weaker animals and organisms

Grooming: To clean and make neat

Habitat: The place where an animal or plant naturally lives

Hybrid: A mix of two animals or plants of different species

Litter: The name given to cubs born at one birth

Lunge: To suddenly jump forward or run towards

Marsupial: Those mammals where the mothers carry their young around in a pouch

Predators: Animals that prey on other animals for food

Prehistoric: That part of history for which no written record is available

Prey: An animal that is hunted by another animal for food

Pupil: The small opening in your eye that lets in light

Retractable: Something that can be pulled back

Rosette: A marking that looks like a rose

Saharan regions: The desert regions of North Africa

Savannah: The grasslands of Africa. In North America they are called the prairies and in South America they are called the pampas

Species: A group of animals or plants that have similar characteristics

Spruce forests: A forest made up of a kind of evergreen pine tree

Stalk: To chase prey silently

Stealth: To do something secretly or quietly

Tissue: A group of cells in any living being

Index